Tundra Biome

by Grace Hansen

abdopublishing.com

Published by Abdo Kids, a division of ABDO, PO Box 398166, Minneapolis, Minnesota 55439.

Copyright © 2017 by Abdo Consulting Group, Inc. International copyrights reserved in all countries. No part of this book may be reproduced in any form without written permission from the publisher.

Printed in the United States of America, North Mankato, Minnesota.

052016

092016

 THIS BOOK CONTAINS RECYCLED MATERIALS

Photo Credits: iStock, Shutterstock

Production Contributors: Teddy Borth, Jennie Forsberg, Grace Hansen

Design Contributors: Laura Mitchell, Dorothy Toth

Cataloging-in-Publication Data

Names: Hansen, Grace, author.

Title: Tundra biome / by Grace Hansen.

Description: Minneapolis, MN : Abdo Kids, [2017] | Series: Biomes | Includes bibliographical references and index.

Identifiers: LCCN 2015959105 | ISBN 9781680805055 (lib. bdg.) | ISBN 9781680805611 (ebook) | ISBN 9781680806175 (Read-to-me ebook)

Subjects: LCSH: Tundra ecology--Juvenile literature.

Classification: DDC 577.5--dc23

LC record available at http://lccn.loc.gov/2015959105

Table of Contents

What is a Biome?

A biome is a large area. It has certain plants and animals. It also has a certain **climate**.

4

desert

forest

freshwater

marine

grassland

tundra

5

Tundra Biome

Tundras are biomes. There are two main kinds. Arctic tundras are located far north.

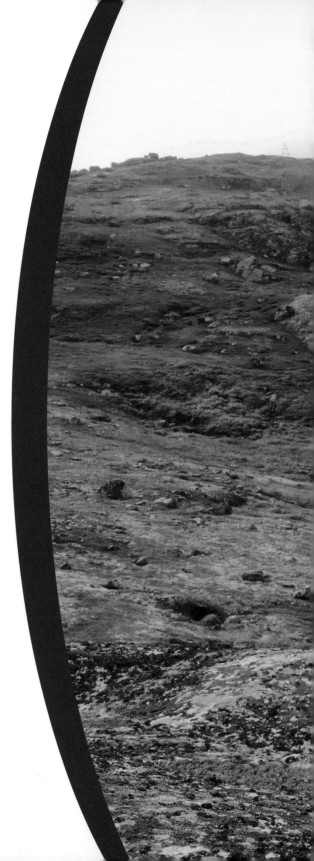

6

7

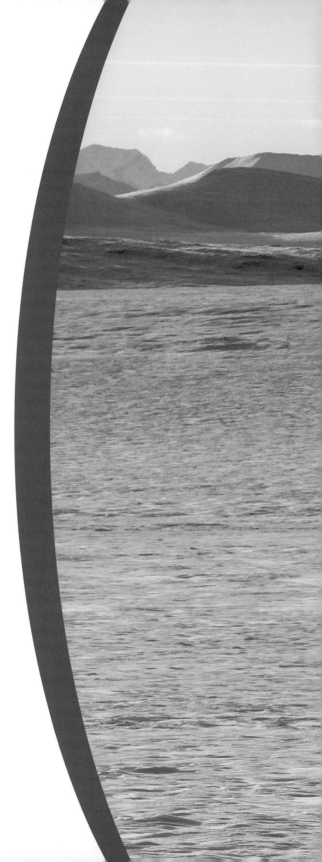

Arctic tundras are very cold.

Their winters are very long.

The usual temperature in

winter is -30° F (-34.4° C).

Summers are very short.
Summers allow this biome
to **maintain** life. Temperatures
reach 54° F (12.2° C). The
sun shines all day and night.

Alpine tundras are found on mountains. They are very cold and windy. The usual temperature is below 10° F (-12.2° C). Summers can warm up to 50° F (10° C).

13

Plants

Trees do not grow on tundras. This is due to cold, wind, and lack of water. Also, the **elevation** is too high on alpine tundras.

Low shrubs grow on tundras.

Mosses, grasses, and flowers
grow, too.

Animals

The arctic tundra is a hard place to live. Only certain animals can survive. Arctic hares and polar bears live there. Arctic foxes and other animals live there, too.

18

Animals living in alpine tundras are also special. They must live high up in mountains. Mountain goats and elk live in alpine tundras.

Things You Might See in a Tundra Biome

Arctic tundra

Alpine tundra

caribou

alpaca

snowy owl

andean condor

bearberry

moss campion

22

Glossary

climate – weather conditions that are usual in an area over a long period of time.

elevation – height above sea level.

maintain – to provide support or upkeep of.

23

Index

abdokids.com

Use this code to log on to abdokids.com and access crafts, games, videos, and more!

Abdo Kids Code:
BTK5055